Guy Waters is one of
and able academicia
the church. This pri
and sure-footed guide that is conversant with
the latest scholarly issues. By reading this book,
you will be grounded in this most important of
doctrines and your faith will be enriched. If you
are not absolutely certain about the biblical way
of justification with God, then reading the Bible
with this book in hand is your most urgent need.

Richard D Phillips
Senior Minister
Second Presbyterian Church
Greenville, South Carolina

Waters offers a concise yet extremely helpful
treatment of what Scriptural justification is,
its practical value in the Christian life and how
the doctrine is being challenged in our present
day. I won't hestitate to give this little book to the
university students under my pastoral care.

Aaron Messner
College Chaplain
Covenant College
Lookout Mountain, Georgia

those rare treasures a serious
whose feet are grounded in
on justification is a clear

BEING MADE
RIGHT WITH GOD?

GUY WATERS

Dr Guy Waters is Associate Professor of New Testament at Reformed Theological Seminary, Jackson, Mississippi. He has published a number of books including *Justification and the New Perspectives on Paul* (P&R Publishing).

Copyright © Guy Waters 2010

ISBN 978-1-84550-615-5

10 9 8 7 6 5 4 3 2 1

First published in 2010
by
Christian Focus Publications,
Geanies House, Fearn,
Ross-shire, IV20 1TW, Scotland
www.christianfocus.com

Cover design by Paul Lewis
Printed by Norhaven A/S, Denmark

Contents

Preface 7

1. Justification Defined 11

2. Justification Applied 39

3. Justification Undermined 67

PREFACE

The late Dr John H. Gerstner tells the story of a talk he once gave on the Bible's teaching on justification. A reporter for the local newspaper was present and wrote a story about the talk. Much to Dr Gerstner's surprise, the story reported that the subject of the talk had been 'Just A Vacation'!

The language of justification is increasingly foreign to the secular Western mind. It has not always been that way. When the Reformation burst upon Europe in the sixteenth century, the doctrine of justification by faith alone coursed through the church with a power and effect not seen since the apostolic age. Awakened to the tyranny of a system for salvation that could not deliver what it promised, men and women discovered the freedom that the gospel of grace alone brings to sinners. Some of them willingly sacrificed property, homes, families, and their own lives because of their commitment to this doctrine.

Is justification by faith alone a relic of church history? For the twenty-first-century person, is it simply a way to explain the seismic political and intellectual shifts taking place in Europe a half millennium ago? To understand the otherwise incomprehensible actions of premodern persons? What relevance could it possibly have to modern people living in a modern age?

Put aside the word 'justification' for a moment. Give some thought to what that word is trying to say. There is a holy and just God. There is our sin. There is our accountability to God for our sin. There is a place where sinners go for punishment and never leave. In that word are dark and sober realities.

But there is something else in that word. There is the love of God the Father for sinners – as rich and as deep as it is incomprehensible. There is the Son of God stooping an infinite distance to come into this world – one who was born to die. There is the self-giving of Jesus Christ at the cross. There is the Spirit of Christ, uniting the sinner to the Savior, and clothing the sinner in 'righteousness divine.' Out of the darkness and shadows emerge beams of light.

These realities concern us as human beings – whether we live in the twenty-first century, or the sixteenth, or the first. The Bible, which teaches the doctrine of justification by faith alone, was written to speak to people in all generations. In the pages that follow we are going to consider what God has to say in the Bible about justification.

In this little work, we have three related goals. First, we will get a handle on what justification is ... and is not. Second, we will see that justification is a practical doctrine. It affects the way that believers live every day – how we relate to God, to ourselves, to others, and to the trials of life. Third, we will look at something that has been getting attention in the church over the last few years – the 'New Perspective on Paul.' What is it? What does it have to say about justification?

The first two chapters of this book began as lectures delivered before the Church Society in Hoddesdon, Hertfordshire, UK, at their 2006 Conference, 'The Gospel of Grace.' I reiterate my thanks to the Church Society both for their invitation to me and for their warm Christian hospitality. I especially wish to thank my generous and gracious hosts, the Rev. and Mrs George Curry, and the Rev. and Mrs David Phillips.

The third chapter of this book began as lectures delivered before the Grace Presbytery of the Presbyterian Church in America in Hattiesburg, Mississippi, in September 2008, and at the Sola Scriptura Ministries International Conference in London, Ontario, in November 2008. Both Grace Presbytery and Sola Scriptura Ministries hosted me superbly. I am especially grateful to the Rev. Stan Layton and Mr Heinz Dschankilic, for their sacrificial and hospitable labors on my behalf.

In revising these lectures for publication, I have benefited from the editorial assistance of Messrs. Anthony Pyles and Nicholas Reid, and the Rev. James T. O'Brien. I especially wish to thank Ms Rebecca Rine for her careful, thoughtful, and patient editorial labors with this work.

I dedicate this book to the memory of the late Dr John H. Gerstner, who so tirelessly explained and defended the doctrine of justification by faith alone, and from whose writings and recorded lectures and sermons I and many others have benefited immeasurably.

1.

JUSTIFICATION DEFINED

Introduction

What does the Bible say about justification? The Bible speaks of justification in many places (e.g. Gal. 2, 3; Rom. 3, 4, 5, 8; James 2). It is tempting to jump directly into a definition of justification. Before we do that, however, we need to look at the background to the Bible's teaching on justification. The Scripture tells us that justification is God's 'solution' to our 'problem' of sin. We will first examine the problem that occasions justification. Then, we will be in a better position to understand justification itself.

The Problem

Why Begin Here?

The *problem* that occasions justification is sin. Why, one may ask, should a treatment of justification begin with sin? What does sin have to do with justification? Could we not skip over sin and simply begin discussing justification? The nineteenth-century Reformed author J.C. Ryle addresses precisely this issue in the opening lines of his classic work, *Holiness*.

> The plain truth is that a right knowledge of sin lies at the root of all saving Christianity. Without it such doctrines as justification, conversion, sanctification, are 'words and names' which convey no meaning to the mind ... Dim or indistinct views of sin are the origin of most of the errors, heresies, and false doctrines of the present day. If a man does not realize the dangerous nature of his soul's disease, you cannot wonder if he is content with false or imperfect remedies. I believe that one of the chief wants of the Church in the nineteenth century has been, and is, clearer, fuller teaching about sin.[1]

Ryle's wise comments apply no less to the twenty-first century than they did to the nineteenth. Let us suppose that a person goes to the doctor with an aggressive form of malignant cancer and that the doctor misdiagnoses the problem as a cold. Not only is this doctor's prescribed remedy unlikely

---

1   J.C. Ryle, *Holiness: Its Nature, Hindrances, Difficulties, and Roots* (2nd ed.; 1883; repr. Grand Rapids: Baker, 1979), p.1, 1-2.

to help the patient, but the patient will remain in mortal danger. Misdiagnosis can be fatal.

Ryle reminds us that this principle is also true spiritually. If we water down, compromise, or simply ignore the Scripture's radical diagnosis of the human condition, then we are hardly in a position to receive, much less appreciate, the only prescribed remedy for that problem. This is why any understanding of the Bible's teaching on justification must begin with a study of sin.

Many people today, even people in the church, look at most human beings as basically good people who sometimes do bad things. Some of us, they say, do more bad things than others. Those of us whose good works outnumber or outweigh our bad works will enjoy the favor of the Deity. Those of us whose bad works outweigh our good works will suffer the displeasure of the Deity.

Of course, most people believe that they are good. They believe that their track record of performance is good enough to receive the blessing of God. To be sure, there are some who will fall short. Those who will meet the divine displeasure, however, are notoriously wicked criminals and tyrants – the kind of people we read about in the newspapers and see on the evening news.

This is not to say that people who have this outlook on humanity can have no sense of divine mercy. They may admit that the Deity is favorably inclined to receive and to accept individuals who, though not perfect, are basically good. They may presume that the Deity graciously overlooks their transgressions and failings. But the prevailing basis of the Deity's acceptance of them is the life lived.

In theological terms, what we have just described is a doctrine of justification by works. This doctrine says that a person is accepted before God on the basis of his performance. God rewards that person with life and blessing because that person's life merits that reward. It is as though Adam had never fallen, and sin had never entered the world through Adam. The prevalence of this doctrine shows how deeply engrained the principle 'do this and you will live' (Lev. 18:5; Rom. 10:5; Gal. 3:12) is upon the hearts of Adam's descendants.

The Bible's testimony, however, is that a sinner's track record can never merit the favor of a holy God. On the contrary, that track record can only bring him under the condemnation of God. The Bible explains how this is so in two ways. First, it gives us an *empirical* assessment of the human condition. It surveys the human landscape and gives us God's assessment of human behaviors, words, thoughts, choices, and desires. Second, it gives us what we might call an *historical* account of the human condition. The Bible answers the questions, 'Why are we the way that we are? Why is it that people are so attached to sin?'

The Empirical Assessment

One of the most extensive surveys of human sinfulness is in the opening chapters of the Epistle of Paul to the Romans. Paul summarizes his survey at Romans 3:9-11, 'What then? Are we Jews any better off [than the Gentiles, or non-Jews]? No, not at all. For we have already charged that all, both Jews and Greeks, are under sin, as it is written: "None is righteous, no, not one; no one understands; no one seeks for God."'[2]

Paul comes to this conclusion by focusing on the Gentiles, on the one hand, and on the Jews, on the other. Paul insists that all people, even the Gentiles, know God through the world that God made (Rom. 1:20, 21). Furthermore, their consciences bear witness to the righteous law of God (Rom. 2:14-15). God has given all people an innate sense of right and wrong. They are aware that wrongdoers 'deserve to die' (Rom. 1:32).

One might think that people who know the difference between right and wrong and who know the consequences for wrongdoing

---

2   Unless otherwise indicated, quotations from Scripture are taken from the English Standard Version.

would live the way that God wants them to live. After all, many in our world today tell us that education is the solution to society's problems.

Paul's statements are a splash of cold water in the face. He calls people 'haters of God' (Rom. 1:30). Hating God, they hate one another (Rom. 1:29-31). What's more, they are 'inventors of evil' (Rom. 1:30). Never satisfied, always bored, they are in a frenzied race to find newer and newer ways to sin. Rather than making them better, the knowledge of God leaves sinners worse off than if they had never known God in the first place.

What about the Jews? Perhaps they are better off than the Gentiles. After all, they have received the Torah, the law of Moses. They have received the sign of God's covenant, circumcision. Surely they must be in a better position than the Gentiles.

Paul's assessment of the Jews is sobering. Simply having the law or receiving circumcision cannot put a person into God's favor. It is not that Paul discounts the law and circumcision (Rom. 3:1). They are valuable, but they cannot deliver a sinner from the righteous judgment of God. The Jew who sins will be held accountable for his sins (Rom. 2:1-10). If he perfectly and continually observed all the requirements of the law, then God could accept him on that basis

(Rom. 2:13). The problem, of course, is that he does not keep the law perfectly. Simply 'hearing the law' will be of no value to bring him into God's favor. 'Doing the law' is what counts.

Is Paul singling out Jews for bad treatment? Is this anti-Semitism? No. Paul, after all, is a Jew himself. He loves his people greatly (see Rom. 9:1-3). He is addressing a problem that uniquely arises within God's people. We could put Paul's point in contemporary terms. Let us say a person is baptized, faithfully attends church services, and daily reads the Bible. Paul is saying that these things cannot bring that person into God's favor. They can't bring him into God's favor because God requires a perfect record to enter into His favor (Rom. 2:13, 26, 27), and no member of God's people can produce that perfect record.

God shows no favoritism, Paul says. He will not give the Jews special treatment simply because they are His chosen people. God is just. He has one standard for every human being, Jew or Gentile. In fact, if a Gentile were ever to keep the law perfectly, he would rise up to condemn the Jew (Rom. 2:25-29)!

So where does this put us? Paul tells us that just as perfectly keeping the law would bring life, sin brings death (Rom. 6:23). What does the law do for sinners? It cannot bring life. Instead, the law makes us aware of our sins (Rom. 3:20).

Paul is not alone in his overview of the human condition. The apostle James says 'We all stumble in many ways, and if anyone does not stumble in what he says, he is a perfect man, able also to bridle his whole body' (James 3:2). Solomon testifies, 'There is no one who does not sin' (1 Kings 8:46) and 'Who can say, "I have made my heart pure; I am clean from my sin?"' (Prov 20:9). Eliphaz asks, 'What is man, that he can be pure? Or he who is born of a woman, that he can be righteous?' (Job 15:14), even as Job asks, 'Who can bring a clean thing out of an unclean? There is not one' (Job 14:4). David declared that he was 'brought forth in iniquity and in sin did my mother conceive me' (Ps. 51:5). In the days of Noah, God looked upon humanity and 'saw that the wickedness of man was great in the earth, and that every intention of the thoughts of his heart was only evil continually' (Gen. 6:5). Jesus declared, 'Out of the heart come evil thoughts, murder, adultery, sexual immorality, theft, false witness, slander' (Matt. 15:19).

The Scripture is united in its testimony to human sinfulness. It looks upon the human landscape, in various times, places, and cultures, and doggedly observes one fact: people sin. Think for a moment what the law requires of you and me. Jesus puts it this way, 'You shall love the Lord your God with all your heart and with all your soul and with all your strength and with all your mind' (Luke 10:27). Jesus says that God requires perfect love for Him in every thought, choice, desire, and action. Let me ask you a question. Be honest – really honest. Have you ever for a moment loved God this way? If you answered truthfully, you have said, 'No, I don't love God this way. I don't keep the law of God, and I never have.' If you have come to the point where you see that sin clings to your every thought, choice, desire, and action, then you understand your sin-problem.

The Historical Explanation

Why are we this way? Why is it that 'none is righteous, no, not one' (Rom. 3:10)? Were people always this way?

The Scripture gives us the answer to these questions. We are the way that we are because of Adam. We are each guilty of Adam's first sin, and we are therefore each born corrupt. The apostle Paul states this truth most succinctly at 1 Corinthians 15:22, ('… in Adam all die,') but develops it most thoroughly at Romans 5:12-21.[3] In this passage, Paul declares, 'Therefore, just as sin came into the world through one man, and death through sin, and so death spread to all men

---

3   The following discussion has been adapted from Guy Prentiss Waters, *Justification and the New Perspectives on Paul* (Phillipsburg, N.J.: P&R, 2004), pp. 181-3.

because all sinned...' (Rom. 5:12). He traces the origin of sin in all people, excepting Jesus, to the 'one sin' of the 'one man.'

Paul is thinking about the sin of Adam in the Garden of Eden (see Gen. 3:1-7). In the verses following Romans 5:12, Paul wants to be sure that we do not misunderstand what he is saying. When Paul says 'all sinned' (5:12), he is not saying that we are sinners because we have followed in the footsteps of Adam by choosing to sin also. People are not born good and then led astray because they are exposed to countless bad examples. This is why Paul says that 'death reigned from Adam to Moses, even over those whose sinning was not like the transgression of Adam' (5:14).

So we see that sin and death did not enter the world because people imitate Adam's bad example. Yet, we have still not answered the question of where sin and death originate. Paul tells us that Adam's descendants, excepting Jesus, were held responsible for Adam's sin. The guilt of Adam's sin was transferred or 'imputed' to Adam's posterity. This is what Paul says at Romans 5:18, 'One trespass led to condemnation for all men,' and at Romans 5:19, 'For as by the one man's disobedience the many were appointed sinners' (author's translation).

Paul presses this point throughout this passage. From the *one* man, Adam, and his *one* sin has come 'death' (5:15, 17) and 'condemn-ation' (5:16, 18). We are dead and condemned because Adam's descendants were appointed sinners (5:19). Death and condemnation did not come, Paul argues here, because of our individual wrongdoing. In fact, they came independently of our activities. They came because of the sin of Adam.

This raises the question, 'Why is Adam's sin *our* sin? Is it fair that God should punish *me* for something that someone else did?' This is an important question. God's integrity is at stake.

The answer to the question of fairness is, 'yes, it is fair for God to transfer the consequences of Adam's sin to you and to me.' Why? To answer that question, we need to see that the Scripture teaches that God established a union between Adam and his descendants, excepting Jesus. This is something different than the biological union that Adam has with every human being. This union is what we might call a representative union. God set Adam apart to represent his descendants. He stands in for them in such a way that his actions become their actions. Let us suppose that Adam had obeyed God in the Garden of Eden. God would have counted that obedience to be our obedience. From birth, we would have lived in God's favor. We would never have known sin. But Adam didn't obey. Adam sinned. That is why God counted Adam's sin to be our sin.

So why was it fair for God to count Adam's sin to be our sin? God was just in establishing this representative union between Adam and his descendants, excepting Jesus. He is our Sovereign Maker and we are His creatures. He is free to do with us as He pleases. And if God was just in establishing this relationship, He was certainly just in transferring Adam's action to those in relationship with Adam – people like you and me.

You may have noticed something in our discussion. We have said that the union between Adam and his descendants excluded Jesus. There is one descendant of Adam who is not 'in Adam' – Jesus. As a result, the consequences of Adam's sin were not transferred to Jesus. Jesus, to be sure, is a true and complete human being. He is, according to His humanity, descended from Adam through Mary, His mother. But because He was conceived by the Holy Spirit and not by a human father, Jesus was not 'in Adam.' This is why the sin of Adam was not imputed to Jesus.

So Jesus was and is truly and fully human. Why is it that He was not 'in Adam'? It is because He is the 'Second Adam' or 'the Last Adam' (see 1 Cor. 15:47; 1 Cor. 15:45). Because He is the Second Adam, He is uniquely qualified to save sinful sons of Adam. Because He is not 'in Adam,' He does not need the salvation that you and I need. Because He is a representative person, His work can deliver those whom He represents. He can save sinners from their sin!

We are now prepared to answer the question – why is humanity universally depraved? Why is it that we are by nature sinners? The answer is that from the moment of our conception, we are guilty of Adam's first sin. We are condemned independently of our own activity. It is because of the guilt of this one sin that we are sinners from conception. Just as Adam was punished for his first sin with a sinful nature, God justly punishes us for the guilt of Adam's sin by creating us with a depraved nature.

The tragedy of our condition is that we are unable to change ourselves. We are 'dead in trespasses and sins' (Eph. 2:1). Spiritually speaking, there is no life or health in us. We have as much ability to move towards God as a corpse has strength to arise from the grave.

If there is any hope for salvation, it must come entirely from outside of us. It must come solely on the initiative of God. The good news of the gospel is that God, in His sovereign mercy, has purposed to save sinners through His Son, Jesus Christ.

Salvation answers the problem of sin. Now that we better understand our problem, we can better understand salvation. One important aspect of salvation is justification.

Justification
Getting Some Definition

> Q. What is justification?
>
> A. Justification is an act of God's free grace
> unto sinners, in which he pardons all their
> sins, accepts and accounts their persons
> righteous in his sight; not for anything
> wrought in them, or done by them, but
> only for the perfect obedience and full
> satisfaction of Christ, by God imputed to
> them, and received by faith alone.
>
> *Westminster Larger Catechism,*
> *Question and Answer Seventy*

What is justification? To answer this question, we will call upon the Westminster Larger Catechism to help us understand the Bible's teaching on this doctrine. The Westminster Larger Catechism is a survey of biblical teaching in question-and-answer format. Drafted by British pastors in the seventeenth century, the Westminster Larger Catechism, along with the Westminster Shorter Catechism and the Westminster Confession of Faith, is the confessional standard of many Presbyterian churches today.

Justification is an 'act.' It is a courtroom verdict. We are the defendants, and charges have been filed against us. The judge passes his verdict. There are only two verdicts available to the judge. One of these verdicts is 'condemned,' and the other is 'justified.' If we are 'condemned,' then the judge has pronounced us 'guilty.' If we are 'justified,' then the judge has pronounced us 'righteous.'

God's courtroom is both like and unlike human courtrooms. In both God's courtrooms and human courtrooms, the defendant may be found 'guilty.' But whereas in a human courtroom, the defendant may be found 'innocent' (free from blame), in God's courtroom, the defendant may be found positively 'righteous.'

We see these two mutually exclusive verdicts ('condemned' / 'justified') paired at Romans 8:33-34, 'Who shall bring any charge against God's elect? It is God who justifies. Who is to condemn? ....' Romans 5:16 shows us the same thing, 'For the judgment following one trespass brought condemnation, but the free gift following many trespasses brought justification.'

It is important to stress that by 'justification' the Scripture means a verdict that God declares concerning us. Justification is not a change that God makes in us. In fact, it is not even the combination of a verdict and an inward change. Justification is strictly a legal declaration.

Justification is an 'act,' a verdict. What is God declaring about the justified person? He is declaring two things. First, all our sins are pardoned. Even though we are guilty of sin, God forgives us. Second, we are righteous persons. Let us look at each of these two parts of justification. If we look carefully, we will see that each part corresponds to a specific aspect of our problem as sinners.

Our first problem is that we have violated the law of God. As transgressors we are subject to the penalty of the law. One word that the Bible uses to describe the law's penalty is 'curse.' As sinners we stand under the curse of the law, 'For as many as are of the works of the Law are under a curse; for it is written, "Cursed be everyone who does not abide by all things written in the Book of the Law, and do them"' (Gal. 3:10 quoting Deut. 27:26). Christ, however, has redeemed us from the curse of the law, having become a curse for us (Gal. 3:13). In other words, on the cross, Christ took His people's curse upon Himself. He answered all that God's justice demanded of them.

God therefore does not count the sins of God's people against them, and He justly pardons or forgives all their sins. This is why David says, 'Blessed are those whose lawless deeds are forgiven, and whose sins are covered; blessed is the man against whom the LORD will not count his sin' (Rom. 4:7-8 quoting Ps. 32:1-2).

The beauty of justification is that believers do not receive the pardon of only *some* of their sins.

Rather, God has 'forgiven us all our trespasses' because of what His Son did on the cross (Col. 2:13). This is why believers have assurance that 'if we confess our sins, [God] is faithful and just to forgive us our sins ...' (1 John 1:9).

Notice how the Scripture emphasizes God's justice in the forgiveness of sins (Rom. 3:21-26). If God were to excuse our sins without answering the demands of justice on those sins, God would commit an injustice of cosmic proportions. The Bible emphasizes that the forgiveness of sins is a just act because Christ paid for those sins on the cross. In fact, since Christ has paid for the believer's sins, it would be unjust were God to refuse to pardon them.

There is a second problem that we have. We have failed to obey the whole law. The law says, 'Do this and you will live' (Lev. 18:5; Rom. 10:5). Because we fail to keep the whole law, we are unable to enter into 'life.' To receive pardon is an unspeakable mercy. Pardon, however, is insufficient to bring a person into divine favor.[4] Pardon renders an objectionable person non-objectionable, but it does nothing to commend this person to God.

---

4   To be sure, God set His favor upon a person when He chose that person in Christ before the foundation of the world (Eph. 1:4). By 'favor' here and in some other places in this chapter and this book, I am referring to an elect sinner being reconciled to God through Christ.

Let us illustrate by a mathematical analogy. Pardon removes a person from the negative column and places him at 'zero.' Pardon, however, does not thereby render a person acceptable. It does not transfer him into the positive column.

The glory of justification is that the sinner is declared 'righteous.' In Christ, the justified sinner becomes the 'righteousness of God' (2 Cor. 5:21). Justification means that the 'righteousness of God' becomes the sinner's (Rom. 3:20ff.). In Christ we 'receive ... the free gift of righteousness' (Rom. 5:17). Consequently, the sinner in justification is declared righteous. This is why the apostle Paul pauses, in a discussion about justification, to say 'the righteous shall live by faith' (Gal. 3:11 quoting Hab. 2:4b).

How is it that the sinner can be accepted and accounted righteous before a holy God? We have already seen the Scripture's teaching that the sins of the sinner are imputed to Christ, who answered all the demands of divine justice, fully satisfying divine justice on behalf of His people. That satisfaction is transferred or imputed to the believer. This satisfaction is part of the believer's righteousness in justification.

The Scripture also teaches that the perfect obedience of Jesus Christ is transferred or imputed to the sinner for his justification. Paul writes 'by the one man's obedience the many will be appointed righteous' (5:19). Justification is not pardon only, as precious as the pardon of sins is to the believer. Justification is more. It is the declaration that a sinner is 'righteous' because the obedience as well as the satisfaction of Christ has become his.

Before we consider the 'instrument' of justification, let us ask a question that sometimes arises at this point in the discussion. Why is it that the work of Christ can come into the possession of the believer? Is it right for God to pardon the sins of the justified believer and to declare him righteous because of what someone else has done for him?

The reason that it is right for God to impute the righteousness of Jesus Christ to sinners is precisely the same reason why it was right for God to impute the first sin of Adam to his posterity. That reason is the union that exists between the First Adam and those whom he represents; and between the Second Adam and those whom He represents. In other words, the union between Christ and His people means that God justly imputes their sins to Him and His righteousness to them.

Two passages will help us to see this truth more clearly. The first passage is 2 Corinthians 5:21, 'For our sake he made him to be sin who knew no sin, so that in him we might become the righteousness of God'. Whom does Paul have in mind in this passage? He is thinking of two parties, Christ (5:20) and believers.

Paul tells us that Christ 'knew no sin.' He is affirming the sinlessness of Jesus Christ. Christ committed no sins and did not have a sinful nature. Although Paul does not say it, he assumes that we are sinners. We are sinners by nature as well as by the things that we think, say, and do.

Paul says something that might startle us. God 'made [Jesus] to be sin.' What does the apostle mean? He cannot mean that Jesus became sinful in the sense that He acquired a personal experience with sin. After all, Paul says, He 'knew no sin.'

The clue is found in the phrase 'for our sake.' He was 'made to be sin' because our sins were laid upon Him or reckoned to Him. In other words, our sins were transferred to the one who is personally righteous, so that He is justly reckoned to be sin. Jesus does not, however, thereby personally become a sinner. He is a sin-bearer. It is as a sin-bearer that He is reckoned to be 'sin.' Our sins were imputed to Him.

Paul says more in 2 Corinthians 5:21: 'so that in [Christ] we might become the righteousness of God.' Believers become the 'righteousness of

God.' In what sense does Paul say that we do this? We become the righteousness of God in precisely the same way that God made Christ to be sin. We become the righteousness of God by transfer or imputation. The righteousness of Christ is imputed to the believer even as his sins are imputed to the Savior. Just as Jesus did not become sinful when he was 'made to be sin,' so also we do not 'become the righteousness of Christ' because of a change that God makes in us. To use technical language for a moment, our righteousness in justification is not infused or inwrought. Rather, our righteousness in justification is imputed to us in precisely the same fashion that our sins were imputed to Jesus Christ. This is why this passage has been rightly called the 'Great Exchange' – our sins are exchanged for Christ's righteousness. Christ bears our sins and gives us His righteousness.

Paul not only tells us that this exchange happens, but he also tells us how it happens. He tells us how it happens when he uses the words 'in him.' It is because the sinner is 'in Christ,' in union with Jesus Christ, that his sins are imputed to Christ, and Christ's righteousness is imputed to the sinner. Union is the foundation for imputation. Some have argued that we must choose between union with Christ *or* the imputation of Christ's righteousness to the believer in order to explain justification. The Scripture shows us that this is a false dichotomy. It is precisely because the believer is in union with Christ that his sins are imputed to Christ and that Christ's righteousness is imputed to him.

One other passage where the Scripture helps us to see that the righteousness of Christ is transferred to those in union with Jesus Christ is Romans 5:12-21. Paul tells us that Christ's righteousness is transferred to those whom He represents in precisely the same way that Adam's sin was transferred to those whom he represents. Just as God condemned those in Adam because the sin of Adam was transferred or imputed to them, God justifies those in Christ because the work of Jesus Christ is transferred or imputed to them (see especially Rom. 5:16, 18-19). The transfer of the actions of each representative head takes place in the context of the union that exists between the representative and the represented.

The Instrument of Justification

Let us return to our definition of justification. We have seen that justification belongs in the courtroom. Justification is a verdict pronounced by the Divine Judge. The verdict concerns sinners who already stand justly condemned for their sins. In this verdict, God declares that all of their sins are pardoned. He also declares that they are righteous persons. The reason that God makes this verdict is that the righteousness of Jesus Christ belongs to them. God has transferred the righteousness of His Son to those persons whom His Son represents.

How do we come to lay hold of the righteousness of Jesus Christ? The Catechism's answer to this question is that the imputed righteousness of Christ is 'received through faith alone.' Faith is the way we receive the righteousness of Christ for justification.

The Bible teaches that we are justified 'through faith.' We are not justified 'because of faith' or 'on account of faith' (see Rom. 3:28, 9:30; Gal. 2:16). Let us think about why this is so. What would it mean if a person were justified 'because of faith' or 'on account of faith'? It could mean that God transfers the righteousness of Jesus in response to our faith. That would make Christ's righteousness to be God's reward for our faith. Or it could mean that our faith in Christ is the reason why God justifies us. That would mean that we have contributed something towards our justification. But the Scripture says that justification is a 'free gift' and comes by the 'grace of God' (Rom. 5:15). We could never be justified *because* of our faith.

Instead we are justified '*by* faith' or '*through* faith.' Faith is the 'instrument' of justification, to use the language of the Larger Catechism. Faith is the way in which we receive Jesus Christ and His righteousness for our justification.

What does the Bible mean when it says that we are not justified 'by works' (Gal. 2:16, Rom. 3:28)? It means that nothing that we have done, are doing, or will do contributes to the basis of God's verdict 'justified.' God does not look on our activity when He justifies us. Instead, He looks only to the perfect work of Jesus. He does not justify us because of what we do. He justifies us because of what Christ did.

We might put it this way: justification is very much by works ... not our works, but the work of Christ! Because justification is based upon the works of Christ alone, our own works are completely excluded from the basis of our justification.

What does faith do in justification? Faith in justification <u>receives</u>. Faith comes empty-handed and receives what God has done in Christ. It is the outstretched hand of the beggar receiving the morsel or coin freely given to him.

Could we say that we have at least contributed faith to the basis of our justification? Is faith a way of sneaking our works in through the back door of justification? No. By definition, faith adds nothing to what Christ has done for His people in justification. When God justifies us, He only looks at what Christ has done. Faith does not supplement what Christ has done for us. Faith, which is itself the gift of God (Phil. 1:29; Eph. 2:8), simply receives what Christ has done for us.

Two passages help us to see what the Scripture means when it says that a person is justified by faith and not by works of the law.

In Philippians 3:9, Paul writes that he does not have 'a righteousness of my own that comes from the law, but that which comes through faith in Christ, the righteousness from God that depends on faith.' Paul here contrasts two 'righteousnesses.' One righteousness is 'from the law' and is our 'own.' This is the righteousness that we produce. It is the righteousness that we claim as our own and that we present to God.

What kinds of things belong to this righteousness? Paul tells us in verses five and six: 'circumcised on the eighth day, of the people of Israel, of the tribe of Benjamin, a Hebrew of Hebrews; as to the law, a Pharisee; as to zeal, a persecutor of the church; as to righteousness, under the law blameless.' In this list, Paul is listing his privileges and accomplishments as a Jew.

The 'righteousness of my own that comes from the law' includes all the accomplishments and privileges that a person might present to God as the reason why he should enter into God's favor. In the twenty-first century, these claims on God's favor might include: membership in an important family; membership in a local church; baptism or confirmation; a good education; service to the community or the church; career success; personal possessions; a good marriage; well-trained children; giving to charitable causes – the list could go on.

Paul then says something remarkable. He calls this righteousness 'rubbish.' It is fit only for the garbage! Why does Paul use such strong language?

He speaks this way because he counts his own righteousness 'loss for the sake of Christ' (3:8-9). The righteousness that comes from God far surpasses anything that Paul or you or I could muster. This righteousness is something that God has done, not something that Paul has done. It is something that God supplies, not something that we supply. This righteousness comes to us 'through faith in Christ.' It belongs to a person not because he has accomplished it or earned it. The righteousness of God belongs to him because he has received it through faith.

Faith has a unique, one-of-a-kind role in justification. Faith receives. Because faith receives, the 'righteousness of God' is God's work and not God's work mixed with our own work. This is why the Reformers insisted that justification is 'by faith *alone*' (*sola fide*). The Roman Catholic Church acknowledges that justification is 'by faith.' It denies that justification is 'by faith *alone*.'[5] This word 'alone' safeguards what Paul is saying in Philippians 3:8-9. Faith and only faith is the way that we receive the righteousness of Christ.

A second passage that shows us what it means that faith receives in justification is Romans 4:4-5, 'Now to the one who works, his wages are not counted as a gift but as his due. And to the one who does not work but trusts him who justifies the ungodly, his faith is counted as righteousness.'

In this passage, Paul outlines two mutually exclusive paths to justification. The first is justification by works. If we want to enter into God's favor on the basis of our own record, Paul says, then what we really want is to receive a wage or recompense from God. We are asking God to give us something that we believe He owes us. We are not asking God for a gift.

The second way, justification by faith, is the exact opposite of justification by works ('to the one who does not work,' Rom. 4:5). This justification has no reference to anything that we do. So far as our justification is concerned, God looks on us as 'ungodly' (Rom. 4:5). What

---

5   *Canons and Decrees of the Council of Trent*, trans. H.J. Schroeder, O.P. (Rockford, Ill.: Tan, 1978), pp. 33-35, 43.

is the hallmark of justification? It is 'trust[ing] him who justifies the ungodly' (Rom. 4:5). The sinner looks beyond himself and rests entirely upon the justifying God.

This is what it means that faith receives. Faith does not belong to the world of wage-earning. It belongs to the world of gift-giving. Faith does not look to what we do. It looks to what God has done in Christ. Faith lays no claim on God. It rests entirely on His sovereign mercy displayed in the gospel of Christ.

Conclusion

In this chapter, we have surveyed the Bible's teaching on justification. We have seen that it is impossible that sinners could produce a right-eousness that would bring them into the divine favor. The good news of the gospel is that the Second Adam has done what dead sinners could not do. By faith alone, we receive and rest upon Christ and His righteousness for our justification. It is in *this* righteousness that the child of God boasts and glories.

What does this marvelous truth mean for the Christian life? If the justified sinner really understands what Christ has done for him in justification, what will this mean for the way in which he lives in the here and now? We will take up these questions in the next chapter.

2.

JUSTIFICATION APPLIED

Introduction

In the Epistle to the Galatians, Paul uses a fascinating word to describe the state of the justified believer: 'freedom.'

> For freedom Christ has set us free; stand firm therefore, and do not submit again to a yoke of slavery. Look: I, Paul, say to you that if you accept circumcision, Christ will be of no advantage to you. I testify again to every man who accepts circumcision that he is obligated to keep the whole law. (Gal. 5:1-3)

To many in the West, the word 'freedom' evokes precious political liberties. We think of *Magna Carta* or the Declaration of Independence. Those of us who enjoy this kind of freedom should be grateful for it. But when the Scripture speaks of the liberty or freedom of the Christian, it is not speaking of political freedom.

Christian freedom belongs to each and every Christian. It is a freedom that Christ has secured and granted uniquely to believers. This is the highest form of liberty that any human being can possibly receive.

Biblical liberty is a two-sided coin. The justified believer has both freedom *from* certain things and freedom *for* certain things. In this chapter, we will reflect on both aspects of our freedom in Christ.

We must issue a caution before we proceed. It is easy to confuse biblical freedom with sinful license. Many believe that biblical freedom means that we are free to live any way that we please. License, of course, is no freedom at all. License is what the Bible calls bondage to sin (Rom. 6:16-17, 19; see also 2 Pet. 2:19).

The Scripture says that we are most free when we are in glad submission to the one, true, living God. Let us now explore what it is *from* which we are free as justified persons, and what it is *for* which we are free. We will then consider some of the tremendous comfort that justification has for the believer in times of distress and disappointment.

Freedom from ...

In the previous chapter, we saw that the Bible teaches that God does not look at our performance when He justifies us. He looks only at Christ's work. The Bible does more than declare these things. It reasons with us and tries to dissuade us from trusting in our own works for justification.

Two such dissuasive passages are found in the Epistle of Paul to the Galatians. False teachers (the 'Judaizers') had infiltrated the church at Galatia. Their error was subtle. They were not telling the Galatians to replace Christ's work for justification with their own observance of the law. They were teaching the Galatians to add their own work to Christ's work for justification.

Paul can hardly believe that the Galatians would even entertain such a proposal (Gal. 3:1-5). But he is confident that in the clear light of day they will not turn their backs on the biblical doctrine of justification by faith alone (Gal. 5:10). This is why he writes a letter to them. He wants them to see two things. First, the justified believer is free from the curse and condemnation of the law (Gal. 3:10-14). Second, he is free from any burden of entering into the favor of God on the basis of his own record (Gal. 5:1-3).

Galatians 3:10-14

In Galatians 3:10, the apostle Paul says that 'all who rely on works of the law are under a curse.' He is not simply saying that those who look to the law to bring them into God's favor will fail this quest. He is saying that those who look to the law to bring them into God's favor will find themselves under the curse of God. They will be under God's curse because they are sinners. The only thing that the law is in a position to do to a sinner is to 'curse' him.

Paul is saying to the Galatians and to us that looking to one's performance in order to secure life is foolish. We will never achieve life by keeping the law. Because of sin, the law speaks the curse of God to sinners.

The apostle does not leave us to despair in this pitiable condition. He does not leave us without hope. But our hope does not lie in ourselves. It lies only in Christ. Paul tells believers that Christ has 'redeemed us from the curse of the law.' How? By helping us to keep the law perfectly so that we can finally enter into God's favor? No, Christ has redeemed us from the curse of the law by taking the curse due to His people for sin at the cross (Gal. 3:13). We can be free from that curse because Christ bore it for sinners. It is only Christ and His work for sinners that can bring a person out of 'curse' and into 'blessing' (Gal. 3:14).

Galatians 5:1-3

Paul tells believers that they have been 'set free' by Christ (Gal 5:1). Their freedom means that they are no longer subject to a 'yoke of slavery.'

What does Paul have in mind by this 'freedom' and 'yoke of slavery'? He is certainly not saying that the Christian is freed from the obligation to keep God's standards for living as they are found in the Ten Commandments (Gal. 5:13-14).

Paul's concern, rather, is with a person who is trying to keep the commandments of the law in order to achieve justification. When Paul speaks of a 'yoke of slavery,' he primarily has in mind the incredible burden resting upon every sinner who has not trusted in Christ for salvation.[1] He is thinking of the impossible task of keeping the law perfectly for justification. Paul calls

---

1   Herman N. Ridderbos, *The Epistle of Paul to the Churches of Galatia* (NICNT; Grand Rapids: Eerdmans, 1953), p. 186; John R. W. Stott, *The Message of Galatians: Only One Way* (BST; Downers Grove, Ill.: InterVarsity, 1968), pp.132-3. Partly Paul has in mind that the New Covenant believer is freed from any burden of having to keep the ceremonial requirements of the Mosaic Law (Gal. 5:2; see also Gal. 4:8-11; Acts 15:10), see John Calvin, *Commentaries on the Epistles of Paul to the Galatians and Ephesians* (repr. Grand Rapids: Baker, 1996), pp. 146-7; and James Fergusson, *An Exposition of the Epistles of Paul to the Galatians, Ephesians, Philippians, Colossians, Thessalonians* (repr. Evansville, Ind.: Sovereign Grace Publishers, n.d.), pp. 84-5.

this a 'burden.' When Christ sets a man free, he relieves him of the burden of keeping the commandments of God so that he may enter into God's favor.

This is why Paul objects so strongly to the Galatians receiving circumcision. In the church at Galatia, if one agreed to be circumcised, circumcision suggested that he was in agreement with the false teachers. The false teachers were saying that a person must be circumcised in order to be a true Christian. They were saying that Christ's work was not enough to justify a person. People had to add their own obedience to Christ's work.

Paul follows this doctrine to its logical conclusions. He tells the Galatians that to receive circumcision on these terms commits them to keep the entirety of the Mosaic law for their justification (Gal. 5:3). He tells them that if they choose to go this route, then they are entirely on their own. 'If you accept circumcision, Christ will be of no benefit to you' (Gal. 5:2). You cannot have it both ways, the apostle is saying. You may try to have either Christ or your own works as the basis of your justification. What you may not have is 'Christ + your works' as the basis of your justification. 'Choose,' Paul says, 'either Jesus Christ or your own performance as the route to your justification.'

This is why Paul goes on to say at verse four, 'you are severed from Christ, you who would be justified by the law; you have fallen away from grace.' We need to be careful when we read this warning. Paul is <u>not</u> saying that truly justified believers have now lost the grace of justification. A truly justified person can never again fall under divine condemnation (Rom. 8:1).

What, then, is Paul saying here? He is saying that any professing Christian who seeks to enter into the favor of God on the basis of his own record has effectively renounced what he once publicly professed himself to be – a sinner justified because of the merits of Christ alone. Paul gives a stern warning to the Galatians: if you sincerely continue to follow the Judaizers (and I hope that you will not), then you will show to yourselves and to the world that you never were justified persons.

Paul is reminding you and me how important the doctrine of justification is to the Christian life. Justification by faith alone sits at the very heart of the gospel. To depart knowingly and willfully from this doctrine is to put one's soul in danger of perishing. This is why Paul opens the body of these letters with these powerful words:

> I am astonished that you are so quickly
> deserting him who called you in the grace of

Christ and are turning to a different gospel
– not that there is another one, but there are
some who trouble you and want to distort the
gospel of Christ. But even if we or an angel
from heaven should preach to you a gospel
contrary to the one we preached to you, let
him be accursed. As we have said before, so
now I say again: If anyone is preaching to you
a gospel contrary to the one you received, let
him be accursed (Gal. 1:6-9).

The Reformer Martin Luther once rightly said
of justification by faith alone that it is 'the article
by which the church stands or falls.' The late
Dr John H. Gerstner adapted Luther's statement
when he said that justification by faith alone is
the article by which *you the Christian* stand or
fall. If we genuinely choose the 'yoke of slavery'
then we will show ourselves never to have known
Christian freedom in the first place.

Freedom To...

We have seen that part of the Christian's
freedom consists in a freedom *from* the curse of
the law, and *from* any burden to keep the law's
demands to enter into God's favor.

We have also seen Paul stress that Christian
freedom is not free. In fact it comes at
a tremendous cost. At the cross, the Son of God
endured the curse and condemnation that was

due to His people. That Jesus Christ willingly bore the curse of the law for sinners renders His sacrifice all the more remarkable. He did not go to the cross against His will. His love for His people drove Him to the cross. This is why Paul can speak of Christ as the one 'who loved me and gave himself for me' (Gal. 2:20).

No Christian can be indifferent or unmoved in the face of the precious truth of the love of Christ for sinners at the cross. This kind of love, Scripture teaches, demands a response. This is why Scripture describes the Christian's freedom in terms of his keeping the law of God. Keeping the law of God is the way that God has appointed for the believer to show his thankfulness to Christ.[2] Let us turn to two passages to help us understand this aspect of Christian freedom.

---

2   The Westminster Larger Catechism states this point well.

Q. 97. What special use is there of the moral law to the regenerate?

A. Although they that are regenerate, and believe in Christ, be delivered from the moral law as a covenant of works, so as thereby they are neither justified nor condemned; yet besides the general uses thereof common to them with all men, it is of special use, to show them how much they are bound to Christ for his fulfilling it, and enduring the curse thereof in their stead, and for their good; and thereby to provoke them to more thankfulness, and to express the same in their greater care to conform themselves thereunto as the rule to their obedience.

Galatians 5:13

In Galatians 5:13, Paul speaks of freedom as something to which believers have been 'called.' He uses the word 'call' to say that Christian freedom carries with it certain responsibilities and obligations.

One responsibility is that we do not abuse our Christian freedom 'as an opportunity for the flesh.' What does Paul mean by 'flesh'? He explains what he means by this word in Galatians 5:16-21. By 'flesh,' Paul has in mind the sin that remains in every Christian.

When Paul warns us that we must 'not use [our] freedom as an opportunity for the flesh,' he is making an important point. In our ongoing battle against sin, we must never look to the doctrine of justification by faith alone as an excuse or pretext for committing sin. We must never think that our freedom from the curse and the condemnation of the law means that we are free from our obligation to keep the law in its entirety. When we see sin, we must flee from it without delay.

Another responsibility of Christian freedom is that we 'through love serve one another.' Notice how Paul defines who the 'one another' are. We are 'brothers' (5:13). We are a family. The Christian family, like my family and your family, has a set of house rules. One key word to our house rules as the family of God is 'love.'

Love is a misunderstood word in our modern
world. Many people equate love with permissive-
ness – allowing people to do whatever they please.
This is not how the Scripture defines love. The
Scripture defines love in terms of keeping God's
law. In the next verse (5:14), Paul says, 'for the
whole law is fulfilled in one word: "You shall love
your neighbor as yourself."' Paul quotes Leviti-
cus 19:18, a passage that Jesus also cites to summarize the second part of the Ten Commandments (see Matt. 22:39). These commandments
show us how God calls us to relate to one another
(Matt. 19:18-19). If we wish to 'love' and 'serve one
another' as 'free' Christians, the apostle Paul says,
then we must do so by obeying God's law.[3]

When Paul says a few verses later that believers are not 'under the law' (5:18), he does

---

3   It is sometimes asked why Paul did not quote the sum-
     mary of the first table of the law, 'You shall love the Lord
     your God with all of your heart, and with all your soul,
     and with all your mind' (Matt. 22:37). The likely reason
     is because Paul is addressing a situation in Galatia where
     professing Christians are in danger of 'biting and devour-
     ing one another' (Gal. 5:15). Reminding the Galatians of
     the second table of the law is therefore a pressing pastoral
     concern. Recall that the Scripture teaches that we cannot
     love others without loving God, just as we cannot love God
     without loving our neighbor (1 John 5:2; 1 John 4:20). To
     reference one of these two summary statements, then, is
     necessarily to reference the other. See Matthew Poole,
     A Commentary on the Holy Bible (3 vols.; repr. Peabody,
     Mass.: Hendrickson, n.d.), 3:657.

not mean that they are free to live as they please. On the contrary, what Christ has done for believers in their justification means that they delight in the moral law and walk by its precepts. We keep the law in the power of the Spirit, by whom we 'live' and 'walk' (5:25). This kind of life, Paul says, is freedom. He is stating what the psalmist had said centuries earlier, 'I will walk at liberty, for I seek your precepts' (Ps. 119:45, NASB).

So why does Paul say that believers are not 'under the law'? He is saying that the work of our Savior means that believers have a whole new relationship to the law. Freed from its curse, we may now delight in and obey the law that we once hated and rejected (Rom. 8:7-8). This, Paul says to the Galatians and to us, is true freedom. Do not accept the counterfeits that the world offers us. Accept the genuine freedom found only in Christ.

James 2:14-26

Another passage that shows us that Christian freedom means 'keeping the law of God' comes from the Epistle of James.

As we study this passage, we meet a difficulty. James says, 'You see that a man is justified by works and not by faith alone' (James 2:24). This passage seems to pose a problem for the doctrine of justification by faith alone. This passage appears flatly to contradict the doctrine.

Critics sometimes draw one of two conclusions from this apparent contradiction. On the one hand, the Protestant doctrine of justification by faith alone is said to contradict the plain teaching of Scripture. James says that the Christian is 'justified by works.' Therefore justification must not be by faith alone, as Protestants have maintained.

On the other hand, others allege that Paul and James are in irreconcilable contradiction. Paul teaches that we are justified by faith alone (Rom. 3:28). James teaches that we are not justified by faith but by works. How can Paul and James both be right?

One does not have to reflect long before he realizes how unsettling this difficulty can be. We seem to be caught between the 'rock' of justification by our own performance and the 'hard place' of biblical errancy.

In our discussion of this passage, we have two objectives. First, we will show that Paul and James are in full harmony. There is no real contradiction between them. Second, we will see James echoing Paul's teaching that the Christian has been set free in order to keep the commandments of God.

Who is (not) justified?

In this passage, James helps us to understand how a professing Christian can know whether he is a justified person. He points out both what does and what does not show us to be justified persons. James is warning us. It is good and desirable that we be assured of our justification. We must not, however, be falsely assured.

James addresses one scenario of false assurance in verse fourteen, 'What good is it, my brothers, if someone says he has faith but does not have works? Can that faith save him?' James has in mind someone who has professed to be a Christian. He claims to have faith, but he lacks good works (see James 2:15-16).

James' phrase 'that faith' means 'a claim to faith that is unaccompanied by good works.' By calling it 'that faith,' he means to separate it from what theologians have called 'saving faith' – genuine faith in Christ that is accompanied by good works.

Is there any value, spiritually speaking, to a claim to faith that is not backed by good works? No. James tells us that this faith is 'dead' (2:17). It is 'useless' (2:20). The apostle uses a graphic image to describe what this faith is like. He tells us that it is like a corpse (2:17, 26). A corpse resembles a living human being, but lacks a principle of vitality. Faith without works is no closer to saving faith than a corpse is to a living human being.

James offers another reason why this faith is of no spiritual profit in verse nineteen, 'You believe that God is one; you do well. Even the demons believe – and shudder!' This faith professes to accept certain propositions. These propositions are not heretical or false. They are orthodox. They are true to biblical teaching. This type of faith may even be accompanied by a strong emotional response to the truth ('and shudder').

Even so, assent to biblical teaching and an emotional response to that teaching do not show that a person is justified. After all, the devils are capable of the same assent and of the same emotional response. James' assumption is that anything that can be true of a devil is no distinguishing mark or trait of a justified child of God.[4]

Let us summarize what James is saying. James tells us that there are three matters that do not prove a person to be justified. They are

4   I have been greatly helped in this treatment of James 2 by Jonathan Edwards, 'True Grace Distinguished From the Experience of Devils,' in *The Works of Jonathan Edwards* (Edward Hickman, ed.; 2 vols.; 1834; repr. Edinburgh: Banner of Truth, 1974), 2:41-50.

his profession of Christianity and membership in the visible church; his assent to biblical teaching; and his emotional response to that teaching.

James is not saying that each of these things is undesirable or bad in itself. He is saying that by themselves they do not show that a person is justified.

What shows a person to be justified? James answers this question in verse eighteen, 'But someone will say, "You have faith and I have works." Show me your faith apart from your works, and I will show you my faith by my works.' James tells us that good works show the truth of our faith. They show that our faith is no 'dead faith' but 'saving faith.'

James does not say that our good works justify us. They are not the reason why we enter into the favor of God. James says that our good works show the truth and reality of saving faith. The presence of good works identifies true faith and sets it apart from its counterfeits.

James simply claims what other biblical writings affirm. We have seen Paul state the same point at Galatians 5:13-14. The apostle John tells us, 'We know that we have passed out of death into life, because we love the brothers' (1 John 3:14). Our Lord Jesus taught, 'Not everyone who says to me, "Lord, Lord," will enter the kingdom of heaven, but the one who does the will of my Father who is in heaven' (Matt. 7:21).

The Scripture speaks with one voice. Our good works do not bring us into the favor of God. But our good works as Christians do identify us as justified persons.

Exhibit A: Abraham

James takes us to the Old Testament to illustrate his point. What is striking about James' illustration is his repeated use of the phrase 'justify by works.' In verse twenty-one, he introduces his example from Abraham's life by saying, 'Was not Abraham our father <u>justified by works</u> when he offered up his son Isaac on the altar?' In verse twenty-four, he concludes his example by saying 'You see that a person is <u>justified by works</u> and not by faith alone.' In verse twenty-five, he offers a corroborating example from the Old Testament book of Joshua, 'And in the same way was not also Rahab the prostitute <u>justified by works</u> when she received the messengers and sent them out by another way?'

What is James saying? Let us draw four observations. First, James calls our attention to Abraham's binding of his son, Isaac, for sacrifice. We find this event recorded in Genesis 22:1-14. Here, we read God commanding Abraham to take his only son to the land of Moriah and to offer him as a human sacrifice. Abraham obeys God in going to the land of Moriah and in preparing to sacrifice Isaac. As Abraham takes up the knife to slay his son, an angel of the Lord prevents him, 'Do not lay your hand on the boy or do anything to him, for now I know that you fear God, seeing you have not withheld your son, your only son, from me' (Gen. 22:12). Abraham's willingness to sacrifice Isaac at God's command is the paramount example of the patriarch's obedience to God. The only reason that Abraham attempted to sacrifice his son was because God told him to do so.

Second, James helps us to understand the importance of Abraham's act. In verse twenty-two, James tells us 'You see that faith was active along with his works, and faith was completed by his works.' Abraham's obedience showed his faith to be the genuine article. That is what James means when he says that Abraham's 'faith was completed by his works.' His faith was no mere claim to faith. Neither was it a simple assent to the truth. His faith was true, saving faith. It produced good works.

Third, James tells us that Abraham's willingness to sacrifice Isaac fulfilled what the Scripture says earlier in Genesis 15:6, 'Abraham believed God, and it was counted to him as righteousness' (quoted at James 2:23). Paul also quotes Genesis 15:6 in order to show that Abraham was justified by faith alone (Gal. 3:6; Rom. 4:3, 22). God imputed to Abraham the righteousness of Christ. Abraham received that righteousness by faith alone.

James is in full agreement with Paul. James does not say that Abraham's sins were pardoned and that Abraham was declared righteous because of his obedience. He says that the Scripture which spoke of Abraham's justification by faith alone (Gen. 15:6) was 'fulfilled' when Abraham later offered Isaac (Gen. 22). When Abraham agreed to sacrifice Isaac, he showed who he already was – a justified person. This is why James says that Abraham's willingness to sacrifice Isaac 'fulfilled' Genesis 15:6. Obedience to the commandments of God, the Scripture says, is the way to know that we are justified persons.

James is simply highlighting a point already evident in the narrative of Genesis. After God prevents Abraham from sacrificing Isaac, He tells Abraham, 'Now I know that you fear God, seeing you have not withheld your son, your only son, from me' (Gen. 22:12). The binding of Isaac was a way for Abraham to show publicly who he really was. It was a way for Abraham to demonstrate that he was a justified person. The good works of the Christian, the apostle James teaches, continue to do precisely the same thing today.

Fourth, this same principle surfaces in a second example that James gives, the example of Rahab (2:25). Rahab was a woman who, like Abraham, had faith in God. We see her faith when she tells the spies 'the LORD your God, he is God in the heavens above and on the earth beneath' (Josh. 2:11). This is no empty confession, James reminds us. She showed the truth of her faith when she risked her own life and the life of her family by giving shelter to the spies of Israel. Her obedience demonstrated the truth of her faith in the God of heaven and earth.

What does James mean when he says that Abraham and Rahab were 'justified by works'? Is James contradicting Paul's statement in Romans, 'For we hold that one is justified by faith apart from works of the law' (Rom. 3:28)? No. Paul and James are writing in perfect harmony with one another. This is evident when we look at how Paul and James define three words: 'works,' 'faith,' and 'justification' (see chart on p. 61).

First, James and Paul define 'works' differently. For James, the 'works' in view are the works of the Christian. These works show the truth of the Christian's faith in Jesus Christ. We might call these works the 'works of sanctification,' or the 'works of the Christian life.' Elsewhere, the Bible speaks of these works as 'fruit' (see Gal. 5:22, Matt. 7:15-20). These are works in which every Christian must abound. With this teaching the apostle Paul is in entire agreement.

The 'works' that Paul has in mind at Galatians 2:16 and Romans 3:28 are altogether different. These works rival or supplement the finished work of Christ as the basis of the sinner's justification. As such, they are categorically forbidden. No sinner ought to look to his own works in order to enter into God's favor. James expresses no disagreement with what Paul says about the place of our works in justification.

Second, James and Paul define 'faith' differently. For James, the 'faith' in view is a claim to faith. A person professes to be a Christian, has membership in the visible church, assents to biblical teaching, and may even have some emotional response to that teaching. 'Not enough!,' says the apostle. True, saving faith must yield good works.

For Paul, the 'faith' by which a sinner is justified is a faith that necessarily produces good works (Gal. 5:6, Rom. 8:1-4). Those good works do not secure God's favor, but those works necessarily accompany saving faith. Paul no less than James rejects any claim to believe in Christ that is unaccompanied by obedience to the commandments of God (Rom. 6:15).

Third, James and Paul define 'justification' differently. Paul by 'justification' has in mind the full pardon of a person's sins, and his being accounted righteous in God's sight. This verdict is based solely upon Christ's righteousness, imputed to the believer and received by faith alone.

James by 'justification' means 'showing that we are in a justified state.' When James says that we are 'justified by works' he means that our good works show us to be justified persons. James is not concerned in this section of his letter with how a person is justified. He is concerned with how a person knows and demonstrates that he is a justified person (see James 2:18). The way that a person knows and demonstrates that he is a justified person is by a life of obedience to God, an obedience that flows from true faith in Jesus Christ.

	James	Paul
Works	Works of the person who has already been justified by Christ's work	Works of the person who is trying to be justified by those works
Faith	Mere claim to faith Not accompanied by good works	Trust in Christ alone for justification Necessarily produces good works
Justification	When we show that we are in a justified state	When we are pardoned, accepted righteous by God solely on the basis of Christ's imputed righteousness

Paul and James are not in contradiction. Paul and James are in full agreement. If we understand this point, then we are better able to appreciate the importance of James' teaching. A claim to faith, membership in the local church, orthodoxy, and emotional responses to biblical teaching are no evidence that a person is justified. The way that a person comes to know that he is a justified person is by a life of obedience to the commandments of God.

James echoes Paul in saying that, while works do not justify us, they are by no means an 'extra' or an optional feature to the Christian life. They are indispensable to the Christian life. The one who has them and knows that he has them may enjoy the comforts of being in a justified state.

Let us conclude this chapter by considering what some of those comforts are.

The Comfort of Justification

In the opening verses of Romans 5, Paul reflects on what justification means to the Christian life. He is especially concerned to apply the doctrine of justification to the suffering Christian. Suffering is something that every Christian must expect to experience (Phil. 1:29, 2 Tim. 3:12). The good news is that the suffering believer's justification means that he has an assurance of peace with God; an enduring joy in the midst of suffering; and an abiding sense of the love of God in Christ. Let us consider each of these precious benefits.

First, Paul tells us that the justified believer has 'peace with God through our Lord Jesus Christ.' To whom does this peace belong? This peace is something that belongs only to the believer, since it is a consequence or implication of our justification (5:1). What kind of peace is this? Since God speaks this peace to those who can expect to suffer, we should not think of this peace in terms of the absence of trial, persecution, disappointment, or loss. For the same reason, we should not equate this peace with inner feelings of serenity and calm. It is a peace that is ours even when we grieve and sorrow in the midst of suffering.

Paul helps us understand this peace when he says it is 'through our Lord Jesus Christ' (Rom. 5:1). This peace is what we might call an objective peace. Once we were under the wrath of God. In Paul's words, we were 'by nature children of wrath' (Eph. 2:3). This is why God says through the prophet, 'There is no peace for the wicked' (Isa. 48:22).

But now, Paul says of believers, 'in Christ Jesus you who once were far off have been brought near by the blood of Christ. For he himself is our peace ...' (Eph. 2:13-14). God has reconciled us to Himself by His Son. If we are resting in the finished work of Christ for our justification, we may have the comfort of knowing that we are at peace with God. Because Christ's work is perfect, complete, and accepted by the Father, and because our peace rests on that work, we will never lose our peace. Our sense of that peace may waver, but our peace itself stands immovable.

In verse two, Paul tells believers that God has caused them to 'stand' in 'this grace,' that is, our justification. God will never let us fall under divine condemnation. The reason we will never lose our peace is not our firm grip on God. Our peace in Christ stands firm because of God's grip on us.

Second, justified persons 'rejoice in hope of the glory of God' (Rom. 5:2). Even though we do not presently experience the glory of God as we one day will, we are assured that it is ours in Christ. God has forged an inseparable link between our justification and our glorification (Rom. 8:30), and what God has put together no creature may put asunder. We should rejoice in that glory here and now because our justification is a title to eternal fellowship and communion with the triune God.

What does it mean to 'rejoice in hope of the glory of God'? It means that our joy is not limited or diminished by our circumstances. Think of the apostle Paul. Paul was in prison when he rejoiced (see Phil. 1:12-14 with Phil. 1:18), and when he commanded believers to rejoice (Phil. 3:1, 4:4). Paul is telling us that our hope puts our trials in perspective. He summarizes the believer's earthly suffering as 'slight momentary affliction' (2 Cor. 4:17).

Paul is not trivializing or demeaning the very serious things we experience in our lives – illness, death, financial loss, problems in our families, to take but a few examples. Paul was a man deeply acquainted with suffering (see 2 Cor. 11:23-29). His own experiences with suffering had not left him callous to his fellow believers' trials.

In fact, his experiences prompted him to apply Christian comfort to his brothers and sisters in distress (see 2 Cor. 1:3-11).

Why does Paul speak of suffering as slight and momentary? It is because for the believer, the worst of earthly suffering pales in comparison with the glory that is his in Christ (Rom. 8:18). It is because God is 'preparing for us an eternal weight of glory' precisely through this 'slight momentary affliction' (2 Cor. 4:17). The world looks at suffering and says: 'Grin and bear it' or 'Whatever does not kill you makes you stronger.' The Scripture calls the believer to look at his justification and to look at his suffering, and then to respond in the only way that he can: to rejoice in the glory that is certainly his in Christ.

Third, the justified believer should be assured that he will never faint under the weight of trial or suffering. 'Hope does not put us to shame, because God's love has been poured into our hearts through the Holy Spirit who has been given to us' (Rom. 5:5). The Holy Spirit has united us to Jesus Christ. He impresses on us an abiding sense of God's love for us in Jesus Christ. Because it is the Holy Spirit who freshly supplies us with these streams of God's love for us, we have further assurance that we will not perish spiritually when we suffer.

In Romans 5, Paul has pointed us to three crucial truths about justification that we need to understand on our Christian pilgrimage to glory. Justification concerns what happened to us when we became Christians, when we passed from condemnation into the favor of God. Justification, however, is not something that the people of God ever outgrow. It never becomes something we can shelve or file away. It is a definitive act based upon the finished work of Christ, but it never ceases to speak to our Christian living in the here and now.

Because the doctrine of justification by faith alone is far-reaching, errors concerning the doctrine are equally far-reaching. Few aspects of the Christian life are unaffected when one departs from the biblical testimony concerning justification. In the next chapter we will consider one important error concerning justification that is facing the church today.

3.

Justification Undermined

Introduction

For much of the church's history, there have been basically two ways of reading Paul's teaching about salvation. The first we might call the 'Augustinian' or 'consistently evangelical' way. This view, as you might be able to tell, is closely associated with one of the greatest theologians of the Christian church, Augustine of Hippo (A.D. 354-430). It did not originate with Augustine, but he was one of the first Christian thinkers to articulate it clearly and relatively fully.[1]

---

1   It would not be until the Reformation, however, that the Reformers would articulate the Augustinian way of reading Paul's teaching about salvation in its most consistent and mature form.

We have been arguing for the Augustinian way of reading Paul in this book. According to Paul, we are sinners by nature. We are not sinners because we sin. We sin because we are sinners. We have no ability to please God. As sinners, we are guilty, that is, we are liable to divine punishment because our sin merits that punishment.

The good news of the Bible is that in Jesus Christ God has shown grace to sinners. 'Grace' is a word that Christians use a lot. Sometimes we do not pause to think about the wonderful reality to which that word points. Grace is the favor of God to the undeserving. Grace is not something that we can merit or earn. In fact, the grace of God is contrary to what we deserve. Neither does God give grace on the basis of what we will do for him as Christians. The grace of God in the gospel is God's unmerited favor to sinners.

When God graciously justifies a sinner, he imputes or reckons or accounts the perfect righteousness of Christ to him. The sinner receives Christ's righteousness by faith alone. Our sins are pardoned and we are accepted as righteous only because of the imputed righteousness of Christ, received by faith alone. God's verdict of justification is complete, final, and irrevocable. For the justified person, there will never again be condemnation.

The second way of reading Paul we might call 'Semi-Pelagian' or 'inconsistently evangelical.' We call this way 'Semi-Pelagian' because it represents a modification of the position of one of Augustine's opponents, the British monk Pelagius (ca. A.D. 354 – A.D. 420 or 440). This view was common in the medieval church. It is also likely the majority viewpoint in the contemporary evangelical church today.

Pelagius taught that human beings by nature are able to fulfill the law of God. We are not born with a nature corrupted by sin. Semi-Pelagianism modifies Pelagius' teaching by acknowledging that sin is a serious problem. Left to itself, sin is a fatal disease that will take the lives of every human being. Sin is not so serious, however, that we are spiritually dead. We are, rather, mortally sick. We have some remaining ability to work with God for our salvation.

Semi-Pelagianism acknowledges the necessity of grace for salvation. Indeed, God takes the first step toward us. Unless we reciprocate with what we have, however, God works to no avail. If we cooperate with God's grace by responding in faith and good works, then these good works become the righteousness by which we are justified. To be sure, Christ's work on the cross is the reason that God pardons our sins for justification. Equally necessary for justification, however, is the righteousness of our good works. On the Augustinian view, the sole righteousness of justification is the atoning death and perfect obedience of Christ, imputed to us and received by faith alone. On the Semi-Pelagian view, we are justified by the atoning death of Christ <u>and</u> our own grace-enabled works. To put it more precisely, Semi-Pelagians teach that we are justified <u>both</u> by the imputed righteousness of Christ <u>and</u> the infused righteousness of Christ. Because the infused righteousness of Christ is ongoing and incomplete in this life, our justification will not be complete until the Judgment Day.

These two ways of reading Paul came to the fore at the time of the Protestant Reformation. Luther, Calvin, and the other Reformers advanced the Augustinian or consistently evangelical way of reading Paul. What came to be known as the Roman Catholic Church taught the Semi-Pelagian or inconsistently evangelical way of reading Paul.

In the last forty or fifty years, some have been calling for a brand new way of reading Paul. This new way of reading Paul has come to be known as the 'New Perspective on Paul' (NPP). It is said to be 'new' because some of its proponents have claimed that the NPP transcends the historical

Roman Catholic – Protestant disagreements on justification.

The NPP began in academia. However, over time, it has made its way into the evangelical and Reformed church. Perhaps its best known proponent in the church is Bishop N. T. Wright. Wright is an accomplished New Testament scholar. Wright is also an officer in the Church of England who identifies himself as both an evangelical and a Calvinist. Wright has the rare ability to communicate effectively both with his scholarly peers in academia and with Christians who do not have specialized theological training. Wright has done good work in affirming the Gospels as trustworthy and reliable historical documents, and in defending the historicity of the resurrection of Jesus Christ.

Because of these reasons and because of Wright's recent claims that the NPP and Reformed theology are in fact compatible with one another, some evangelical Christians have expressed sympathy for the NPP as Wright has articulated and defended it.[2] Our objective in this chapter is to introduce and to respond to

---

2   For Wright's claims that the NPP and Reformed theology are compatible see, for example, N. T. Wright, 'New Perspectives on Paul,' in ed. Bruce L. McCormack, *Justification in Perspective: Historical Developments and Contemporary Challenges* (Grand Rapids: Baker, 2006/ Edinburgh: Rutherford House, 2006), p. 263.

the NPP. We will do so by considering the two topics on which the NPP has had the most to say: Judaism and Justification.

The New Perspective and Judaism

It may be surprising to learn that the NPP began not with the study of Paul but with the study of ancient Judaism, that is, the religion that prevailed among God's people at the time of the New Testament.[3] Prior to the mid-twentieth century, most New Testament scholars saw first-century Judaism as a religion of strict merit. In other words, first-century Judaism was understood to be a religion that had no place whatsoever for grace. One's good works and one's bad works would be put on a scale at the Day of Judgment. If one's good works outbalanced the bad works, then he would go to heaven. If one's bad works outbalanced the good works, then he would go to hell. One's eternal destiny depended entirely upon one's own performance.

This understanding of first-century Judaism is, to be sure, extreme. Jews in the time of the

---

3   This is to distinguish first-century Judaism from the religion of the Old Testament. Both the Old and the New Testaments are united in teaching that salvation is and always has been by grace alone. According to the New Testament, however, many Jews in the first century turned from that teaching of the Old Testament and were trusting in their performance for their acceptance with God.

New Testament did have some understanding of grace. Nevertheless, one may fairly characterize first-century Judaism as a religion of merit.[4] Paul characterizes many of his fellow Jews as trusting in their own performance as the basis of their acceptance with God (Rom. 2:1–3:20).

After World War II, some New Testament scholars began to reassess first-century Judaism as part of a much larger reassessment of Jews and Judaism in light of the events and aftermath of the War. Reading the Jewish literature contemporary to the New Testament, scholars became increasingly aware that 'grace' had a place in first-century Judaism. It was not until E. P. Sanders published his landmark work, *Paul and Palestinian Judaism* (1977), however, that a substantial case had been advanced for the essential graciousness of first-century Judaism.

Sanders exhaustively surveys a great body of first-century Jewish literature. He concludes

---

4   First-century Judaism was a religion of merit but not a religion of strict merit. In other words, it had a place for grace, but was not a fundamentally or essentially gracious religion. It was a fundamentally or essentially meritorious religion. For elaboration, see my 'Introduction: Whatever Happened to *Sola Fide?*,' in Gary L. W. Johnson and Guy P. Waters, eds., *By Faith Alone: Answering the Challenges to the Doctrine of Justification* (Wheaton, Ill.: Crossway, 2007), p. 26.

that first-century Jews shared a common understanding of salvation. Sanders calls this common
understanding 'covenantal nomism.' He famously
summarizes covenantal nomism in this way: one
gets into God's covenant of salvation by grace;
one stays in that covenant by works. Sanders argues that first-century Jews believed in gracious
election, on the one hand; and obedience following that gracious election, on the other hand.
Judaism, according to Sanders, was a gracious
religion because in it the grace of God preceded
human effort. In fact, Sanders had simply established that Judaism was not a religion of strict
merit. He had not established that Judaism was
<u>essentially</u> gracious.

Sanders's conclusion has nevertheless proven
influential. It therefore raises an important
question for the study of Paul. Christians had
long argued that Paul differed with Judaism on
the place of 'grace' and 'works' in justification.
Now Sanders was saying that Judaism was
a religion of grace. What's more, Sanders claimed
that Judaism and Paul agreed on the place of
grace and works in salvation. Their disagreement
lay elsewhere. Where does this put 'justification
by faith and not by works of the law'?

This question brings us to the work of N. T.
Wright. Wright basically accepts Sanders's

conclusions about Judaism. Wright takes up the question why Paul opposed first-century Judaism. Wright tries to explain what the difference was between ancient Judaism and Christianity.

A key passage for Wright is Galatians 2:11-21. In the first part of this passage, Paul is recounting to the Galatians an earlier incident in the church at Antioch. There came a time when 'certain men from James' came from Jerusalem to Antioch (2:11). Prior to their arrival, Jewish Peter had enjoyed table fellowship with Gentile Christians. After their arrival, Paul tells us, Peter 'separated himself, fearing the circumcision party' (2:12). Not only did Peter withdraw from eating at the same table with Gentile Christians, but the rest of the Jewish Christians at Antioch and even Barnabas withdrew as well (2:13). Paul strenuously and publicly objected to this withdrawal because it compelled 'Gentiles to live like Jews,' thus jeopardizing the 'truth of the gospel' (2:14).

In the immediately following verses (2:15-21), Paul proceeds to give a summary of the main issues that he will address in the letter to the Galatians. These issues, following on the heels of Paul's description of the Antioch Incident, thus give expression to Paul's concern over Peter's withdrawal at Antioch. The main issue, Paul says, concerns justification by faith and not by works of the law (2:16).

The question that Wright takes up is how Paul understood Peter's withdrawal from table fellowship to have threatened justification by faith. First, Wright stresses that the main issue at Antioch was not salvation. The main issue at Antioch was one of Christian identity. The question defining the controversy at Antioch was not 'what must I do to be saved?' but 'how do I know who a true Christian is?' The question, for Wright, is whether one should identify Christians by their refusal both to eat food declared unclean by the Mosaic Law and to have table fellowship with those who eat unclean food.

The word that Paul uses to frame this question is, Wright says, 'justification.' When God justifies a person, Wright argues, he declares that person to be a member of the people of God.[5] Justification in the here and now, then, concerns one's identity more than it does one's salvation.

There were for Paul, Wright continues, two competing ways that a person could be 'justified.'

---

5   If God declares a person to be a member of the people of God, Wright argues, He also declares him to be 'in the right,' an already-forgiven sinner. Justification, for Wright, is not the moment when a sinner's sins are forgiven. It is the declaration that a sinner has already been forgiven. The Scripture teaches, however, that justification is the moment at which the sinner's sins are forgiven, Rom. 4:4-6.

The first ('works of the law') says that Christians are identified by keeping the Mosaic Law in its entirety. The second ('faith') says that Christians are identified by faith in Christ. 'Works of the law' do not describe something that Paul's contemporaries were doing in order to merit or earn God's favor in justification. 'Works of the law,' rather, describe the way in which Paul's Christian contemporaries were looking to the Mosaic Law as the mark of Christian identity. 'Faith' in justification is not something that Paul opposes to achievement or effort for justification. 'Faith' is the mark of Christian identity.

Paul is said to devote much of the Epistle to the Galatians to arguing the point that a Christian is not identified as a Christian ('justified') by the badge or marker of law-keeping ('works of the law'). One is identified as a Christian ('justified') by the badge or marker of faith in Christ ('faith'). Peter compromised this truth when he refused to continue eating with Gentile Christians in Antioch. His action was saying that a Christian is in fact identified by law-keeping and not by faith.

There are at least two important implications of Wright's understanding of justification. First, for Wright, justification in the present is primarily about sociology or social boundaries. Justification is not primarily about how a sinner is saved. It primarily concerns exclusion from or inclusion within the people of God. It concerns how one identifies members of the church. Second, if this view is correct, Wright claims, then the five-century-old impasse between Rome and Protestantism on the doctrine of justification has been cleared. On this point at least, the way is open for table fellowship between these two separated bodies.[6]

What are we to make of Wright's proposal? Wright's position hinges on the meaning of three words or phrases: 'works (of the law),' 'faith,' and 'justification.'[7] We will consider each in turn. The benefit of such a study, in addition to allowing us to evaluate Wright's proposal, is that it permits us to rehearse the biblical foundations for the doctrine of justification by faith alone.

Works of the Law

Wright argues that 'works (of the law)' is Paul's way of referring to persons identifying themselves as Christians because of their law-keeping. The biblical evidence, however, points in a different

---

6   Wright, 'New Perspectives on Paul,' 261-2; cf. N. T. Wright, *What Saint Paul Really Said: Was Paul of Tarsus the Real Founder of Christianity?* (Grand Rapids: Eerdmans/ Cincinnati: Forward Movement, 1997), pp.158-9.

7   In the context of justification, 'works' and 'works of the law' mean the same thing.

direction. 'Works of the law' must mean 'deeds done.' Three passages help us to see this point.

The first passage is Romans 4:4-5, 'Now to the one who works, his wages are not counted as a gift but as his due. And to the one who does not work but trusts him who justifies the ungodly, his faith is counted as righteousness.' Paul is speaking here about justification by faith alone. As he does elsewhere in his letters, he contrasts justification by works with justification by faith. Paul tells us what he means by works. He speaks of works in terms of 'wages' or one's 'due.' They are 'not counted as a gift.' As many commentators observe, Paul is using an image from the marketplace to describe 'works' in justification. 'Works' here are deeds done. They are anything that we do for justification. Paul is not concerned in this passage with questions of identity or status.

The second passage is Romans 9:11, 'though they [Jacob & Esau] were not yet born and had done nothing either good or bad – in order that God's purpose of election might continue, not because of works but because of his call ...' Paul is speaking here of election. His point is that God's choice of a person for salvation is not based upon anything that that person does. To put it more precisely, election is not conditioned upon anything in the creature. Election is the eternal, unchangeable, and sovereign choice of God. It is not based upon a person's 'works.' What does Paul mean here by the word 'works'? It is doing something 'either good or bad.' Even though Paul is not speaking about justification in Romans 9, we expect Paul to mean by 'works' in Romans 9 what he meant by 'works' the last time he used this word in the letter (Rom. 4:4, 5, 6). As in Romans 4, 'works' in Romans 9:11 are 'deeds done.'

The third passage is Romans 1:18–3:31. In Romans 3:21-31, Paul articulates the 'solution' to the human problem. That solution is justification by faith alone. In Romans 1:18–3:20, Paul articulates the problem for which justification is God's solution. If Wright is correct, then we expect the problem to center around such matters as boundary markers, group identity, inclusion and exclusion.

That is not how Paul describes our problem. He describes our problem throughout this passage in terms of sin. Paul summarizes the argument of Romans 1:18–3:8 at Romans 3:9-20, which begins 'For we have already charged that all, both Jews and Greeks, are under sin, as it is written, "None is righteous, no, not one"' (3:9-10). Our problem, then, is sin – sin that calls down the wrath of God upon the sinner (Rom. 1:18, 2:5). In Romans 3, Paul describes

God's solution to this problem in terms of justification. Notice how the solution fits the problem. God pardons the sins of the sinner and declares him righteous (Rom. 3:21-23). The sole basis of justification is the meritorious work of the Lord Jesus Christ, climaxing in his propitiatory sacrifice on Calvary (Rom. 3:24-25).

Faith

When we see that 'works' in justification are 'deeds done,' we are in a better position to understand the place of 'faith' in justification. Paul says that 'faith' and 'works' are two mutually exclusive paths to justification: 'yet we know that a person is not justified by works of the law but through faith in Jesus Christ' (Gal. 2:16; see also Rom. 3:28). If 'works' in justification are 'deeds done,' and if 'faith' is the antithesis of 'works' in justification, then 'faith' is 'not doing' or 'receiving.'

This is precisely how Paul describes 'faith' in justification in Rom. 4:4-5, 'Now to the one who works, his wages are not counted as a gift but as his due. And to the one who does not work but trusts him who justifies the ungodly, his faith is counted as righteousness.' To believe is 'not to work.' 'Faith' is the antithesis of 'works' in justification. What then is 'faith'? It is 'trusting him who justifies the ungodly.' As far as justification is concerned, faith sees oneself as ungodly. Faith looks out of oneself to God. Faith trusts the justifying God. Faith receives and rests upon what Christ has done for sinners. Faith contributes nothing, but it draws Christ's imputed righteousness to the sinner.

What Paul refrains from doing here is describing 'faith' in justification in terms of an identity marker, as the badge of membership in the people of God. 'Faith,' rather, describes how God justifies the ungodly. Faith reaches out and apprehends the imputed righteousness of Christ for justification.

Justification

When Paul uses the words 'justify' or 'justification,' he is speaking about the way that God saves a sinner. Justification, first of all, is a legal declaration that a person is 'righteous.' We see Paul teaching this in Romans 8:33-34, 'Who shall bring any charge against God's elect? It is God who justifies. Who is to condemn?' Justification is a legal declaration, a verdict ('charge').[8] It is a declaration that we are no longer under God's condemnation ('Who is to condemn?'). It is therefore a declaration that we are righteous (cf. Rom. 5:16).

---

8   Wright agrees that justification is a legal verdict or dec-
     laration. He does not agree, however, that justification is
     a declaration that the sinner is righteous solely because of
     the imputed righteousness of Christ.

On what basis can a just God make the declaration 'righteous' of an 'ungodly' sinner? Solely on the basis of the 'righteousness of God through faith in Jesus Christ for all who believe' (Rom. 3:22). As we saw in chapter one, Christ is our righteousness for justification (1 Cor. 1:30). Our sins were imputed to Him, and His righteousness was imputed to us (2 Cor. 5:21). Therefore God justly declares us righteous.

Paul does not use the words 'justify' or 'justification' to describe how a person may be identified as a member of the people of God. These words describe God's declaration that a sinner is 'righteous' solely because of the imputed righteousness of Jesus Christ, received by faith alone. That is why Paul can say that believers 'have now been justified by his blood' (Rom. 5:9).

How then do we explain Galatians 2:11-21? We have seen that Wright appeals to this passage in order to support his understanding of justification as God's declaration that a person is already a member of the people of God. This appeal has plausibility because Paul points to Peter's withdrawal from table fellowship with Gentile Christians as compromising the gospel (2:14) and justification by faith alone (2:16).

How, then, did Peter's withdrawal threaten justification by faith alone? Peter withdrew, Paul tells us, because he feared the 'circumcision party'

(2:12). The 'circumcision party' believed that unless a person was circumcised, he could not be saved (see Acts 15:1). Uncircumcised Gentiles, they maintained, could not possibly be regarded as justified persons. When Peter withdrew from table fellowship at Antioch, he was therefore communicating that these uncircumcised Gentile Christians were not justified persons.[9] They were not justified persons because circumcision was necessary for justification, and they had not been circumcised. Peter's action lent credence to the doctrine that a person is justified by something that he does.

Paul responds so strongly to Peter because Peter has compromised the gospel of free grace, the doctrine of justification by faith alone. A person is justified, Paul maintains, not because of anything that he has done or is doing. A person is justified only because of what Christ has done, imputed to him and received through faith alone.

That this is what Paul means by 'justification' at Galatians 2:11-21 is evident from Paul's statements about justification at

---

9　　Paul tells us that Peter, Barnabas, and other ethnically Jewish Christians were 'acting hypocritically' when they withdrew from table fellowship with Gentile Christians at Antioch (2:14). What Paul means is that their action was a betrayal of their principle. Peter really did believe that a Gentile Christian was justified by faith apart from circumcision or any other work of the law (see Acts 10:43). When he withdrew from table fellowship with Gentile Christians, Paul says, Peter was not acting consistently with that belief.

Galatians 3:10-14. There Paul tells us that reliance on the 'works of the law' brings a person 'under a curse' (3:10). Why is this so? Because the 'works of the law' involve doing everything that the law requires (3:10, 12), and no sinner can meet this standard. Therefore, we are under the law's curse. No one can be justified by the law (3:11). The good news of the gospel is that the sinless 'Christ redeemed us from the curse of the law by becoming a curse for us' (3:13). Because Christ took the law's curse for believers, in Christ we now enjoy the blessing of God through faith (3:14).

The New Perspective and Justification

We have already seen how the NPP began with a re-evaluation of first-century Judaism. We have also seen how that re-evaluation has impacted NPP proponents' understanding of Paul's doctrine of justification. Our discussion of Wright's doctrine of justification is at this point incomplete. We have seen Wright speaking of what he calls 'present justification' – God declaring that a person is already a member of the people of God. Wright also speaks of what he terms 'future justification.' Present justification, Wright argues, is something that the believer experiences in this life. Future justification, however, is not something that the believer ultimately experiences until the Judgment Day.

What does Wright mean by 'future justification'? Does the fact that Wright speaks of both a 'present' and a 'future' justification mean that Wright understands justification to be a process that is not complete until the Judgment Day? When we examine Wright's statements on 'future justification,' we see that he understands future justification both to be a process and to be based upon the works of the believer.

> 'Justification, at the last, will be on the basis of performance, not possession.'

> 'Present justification declares on the basis of faith, what future justification will affirm publicly on the basis of the entire life.'

> '[Justification] occurs in the future ... on the basis of the entire life a person has led in the power of the Spirit – that is, it occurs on the basis of "works" in Paul's redefined sense, ... [i.e.] the things that are produced in one's life as a result of the Spirit's indwelling and operation.' [10]

Wright understands the Spirit-enabled works of the Christian to be justifying. They are not merely evidence that one is justified. They are

---

10   Wright, 'Romans' in ed. Leander E. Keck, *New Interpreter's Bible: Acts – 1 Corinthians, Vol. 10* (Nashville: Abingdon, 2002), 440; *What Saint Paul Really Said*, 129; 'New Perspectives on Paul,' 260, 254.

part of the basis upon which God justifies a person. That justification will not be complete until the Judgment Day.

There is one further dimension of Wright's understanding of justification that merits discussion. Wright categorically rejects 'imputed righteousness' as a teaching of the apostle Paul. 'God's righteousness never becomes … an attribute which is passed on to, reckoned to, or imputed to God's people.'[11] For this reason, Wright claims, one may never appeal to the imputed righteousness of Christ as the basis or ground of the sinner's justification. It is impossible, he claims, that Christ's righteousness could be reckoned to the sinner for his justification.

We have seen the Scripture teach, however, that God justifies the sinner because He imputes the righteousness of Christ to him (1 Cor. 1:30, 'And because of him you are in Christ Jesus, who became to us wisdom from God, righteousness and sanctification and redemption;' 2 Cor. 5:21, 'For our sake he made him to be sin who knew no sin, so that in him we might become the righteousness of God'). It is untrue to biblical teaching to say that God's righteousness is never imputed to the people of God. On the contrary, in

---

11 Wright, 'New Perspectives on Paul,' 250. Compare Wright's fuller statement of the same position at *What Saint Paul Really Said*, 98.

union with Jesus Christ, the sinner is robed with the spotless, imputed righteousness of his Savior.

What about Wright's claim that our justification is based upon our performance as Christians? When Paul says that 'a person is not justified by works of the law,' Wright understands the apostle to be excluding the works that a person does before he becomes a Christian. He does not understand Paul to exclude the good works that Christians, in the power of the Spirit, are commanded to do.

Wright certainly departs from the Reformation at this point. The Reformation excluded every human work, whether of the non-Christian or of the Christian, from contributing to the basis of the sinner's justification. Only the works of Christ, the Reformers argued, can justify the sinner. This is why our justification is perfect and complete now. It is not an incomplete process. The pressing question is whether Wright departs from the Scripture. Does the Scripture teach that the works of the Christian are justifying? Is our justification presently complete or incomplete?

When we review passages such as Romans 4:4-5, Romans 3:20, and Galatians 2:16, we see that the Scripture excludes every human work from contributing to the basis of the sinner's justification. There are no exceptions granted. In Romans 4:4, Paul writes 'now to the one who works, his wages are not counted as a gift but as his due.' In Romans 3:20, 'by works of the law no human being will be justified in his sight.' In Galatians 2:16, 'because by works of the law no one will be justified.' It simply does not matter whether the work is performed by a non-Christian or a Christian. All works are excluded.

The Scripture's teaching on the place of faith in justification confirms this point. The Bible consistently teaches that a person is justified <u>through</u> faith or <u>by</u> faith. The Bible never teaches that a person is justified <u>on account of</u> faith or <u>because of</u> faith. This is because what faith does in justification is to receive Christ. Strictly speaking, faith does not justify the sinner. Christ justifies the sinner. Faith must produce good works. Those good works, however, are never justifying.

Do the good works of the Christian have any place in discussions of justification? Of course! We saw in the previous chapter that works are necessary evidences of saving faith. Good works show our faith to be genuine, saving faith. They do not justify us. They are the way that we come to know that we are justified persons. This is what James teaches in James 2:14-26. Justifying faith is a faith that produces good works. In that sense and in that sense alone do our works have a place in justification. Good works, whether done before or after conversion, do not justify the sinner. The good news of the gospel is that Christ's imputed righteousness is sufficient to justify the foulest sinner, and to justify him perfectly and completely now.

Concluding Reflections on the New Perspective on Paul

It may be that you have been reading this chapter wondering, 'What does this have to do with the church? with my Christian life?' These are two excellent questions and they merit careful answers. Let us first think about what the implications of the NPP are for the pastoral ministry. Then we will consider how the issues raised by the NPP affect the Christian life generally.

It is important for those who are serving in the pastoral ministry to understand that the NPP raises a 'gospel' issue. In other words, what is at stake is the clarity and integrity of the gospel and of its proclamation to needy sinners. The NPP raises concerns in two related areas. First, the NPP diminishes sin. According to its view, we are not so fallen that we are unable to contribute to the basis of our justification before God. Second, the NPP diminishes grace. In the NPP,

Christ's work is not so sufficient that we cannot supplement it to be made right with God. For all that the NPP claims to be 'new,' it is in fact quite 'old.' It is a form of the Semi-Pelagianism that has been with the church for many centuries now.

The gospel that the Scripture has given to the church begins with the announcement of the bad news that people are dead in trespasses and sins, having no hope and without God in the world (Eph. 2:5, 12). The good news is that God has sent His Son to do what no mere man could do: to live and to die for sinners so that they might be brought near to God. The God-ordained goal of the gospel is to bring glory to God (see Eph. 1:6, 12; Col. 1:18; Rom. 11:33-36). When we tell people that they are able to contribute something toward their justification, we detract from God's glory in the gospel. If God is to receive the glory that is His due, it must be through the God-exalting, man-abasing gospel that He has entrusted us in the Bible.

What does the NPP have to do with the Christian life? Much in every way! First, we have seen that because of justification, the justified believer has 'peace with God through our Lord Jesus Christ' (Rom. 5:1). She has the assurance that she stands in the grace of justification and will never be permitted to fall into condemnation

(Rom. 5:2). She 'rejoices' in the certain 'hope of the glory of God' (Rom. 5:2). Peace, assurance, and joy – all flow from our justification. If our understanding of justification is compromised, then our grasp of the peace, assurance, and joy that is the believer's through the gospel will be weakened. How can I have a strong sense of peace, assurance, and joy if I believe that my justification depends in the slightest degree upon my performance? On the other hand, if I know that Christ has done everything that God has required for my justification, how could I not know the peace of God; be assured that I will never again stand condemned; and rejoice in my heavenly hope?

Second, the Scripture tells us that we must live the Christian life in grateful remembrance for what Christ has done for us in the gospel. This is how Paul reasons in Romans 12:1-2, 'I appeal to you therefore, brothers, by the mercies of God, to present your bodies as a living sacrifice, holy and acceptable to God, which is your spiritual worship. Do not be conformed to this world, but be transformed by the renewal of your mind, that by testing you may discern what is the will of God, what is good and acceptable and perfect.' Paul has spent eleven chapters in Romans unfolding God's mercies. He now appeals to those same mercies as what should motivate Christians to present themselves as 'living sacrifices' before God.

Whereas the Scripture motivates us to do good works because we have been justified, the NPP calls us to do good works in order to be justified. The NPP puts our works in the wrong column. We are not justified by good works. We are justified so that we might abound in good works. Assured of God's peace, of a firm standing before God, and of the glory that is certainly ours, we have powerful motives to abound in the good works that glorify our great God.

This raises a final question. Is there anything that we can learn from the NPP? Does the NPP have anything to say to the church today? The answer is a resounding 'yes.' Sometimes the rise and spread of error can help the church see areas of biblical teaching that she could teach with greater emphasis or clarity. The NPP reminds us that justification has genuine implications for the life of the church. While the NPP is mistaken to identify the fellowship and unity of the body of believers with justification itself, the fellowship and unity of the people of God are genuinely necessary implications of justification.

Two biblical examples illustrate this point. In Romans 14–15, Paul addresses a problem in the church at Rome. Two groups (the 'strong' and the 'weak') are divided.

Paul calls for them to pursue Christian unity. He not only commands them to pursue unity, but he also shows them how to pursue unity: 'Therefore welcome one another as Christ has welcomed you, for the glory of God' (Rom. 15:7). The pursuit and expression of Christian unity begins with an understanding of the gospel ('as Christ has welcomed you'). Paul, of course, devoted the first eleven chapters of Romans to unfolding how God saves sinners. In the same way that Christ received you, Paul writes, receive others. We are helpless sinners who have been justified by the grace of God, on the basis of the sufficient work of Christ, imputed to us and received through faith alone. Live with one another as those who were, spiritually speaking, less than nothing and who have received everything by the grace of God. Putting this truth into practice is indispensable for Christian unity.

A second passage that shows how the doctrine of justification should inform and shape the life of the church is Eph. 2:1-22. In Eph. 2:1-10, Paul unfolds the riches of salvation by grace alone. He is talking about more than justification, to be sure, but justification is certainly in view. God, who is rich in mercy, has saved dead sinners in His Son. In Eph. 2:11-22, Paul applies this truth to the relationships among Jews and Gentiles in the church. Formerly, Paul writes, Jew and Gentile were separate and at odds with one another. At the cross of Christ, however, God has brought the two together. He has 'reconciled us both to God in one body through the cross, thereby killing the hostility' and 'created in himself one new man in place of the two, so making peace' (Eph. 2:16, 15). We see the apostle directing our gaze to the cross and our justification in order to foster the unity that is ours in the church.

How then do we respond to the NPP? We uphold the glorious gospel of grace in its integrity and clarity. We tell sinners how bad they are and how good God has shown Himself to be in the gospel. We invite men to come to Christ in the way of faith and repentance. We summon them to exchange their 'filthy garments' of sin for the 'pure vestments' of Christ's imputed righteousness (Zech. 3:3, 4).

And then, as justified persons, we live out the truth of our justification, especially in relationship with one another. We show visibly and concretely what it means to be a sinner justified by the grace of God. We live as sinners who have been humbled by a sense of our sin and desert. We grow in the knowledge that we are ever and only debtors to divine mercy. We live in the quiet, humble confidence that we belong to God, that He will never leave us nor forsake us. And in all this we 'rejoice in the hope of the glory of God.'

Christian Focus Publications

publishes books for all ages

Our mission statement –

STAYING FAITHFUL

In dependence upon God we seek to impact the world through literature faithful to His infallible Word, the Bible. Our aim is to ensure that the Lord Jesus Christ is presented as the only hope to obtain forgiveness of sin, live a useful life and look forward to heaven with Him.

REACHING OUT

Christ's last command requires us to reach out to our world with His gospel. We seek to help fulfill that by publishing books that point people towards Jesus and help them develop a Christ-like maturity. We aim to equip all levels of readers for life, work, ministry and mission.

Books in our adult range are published in three imprints.

Christian Focus contains popular works including biographies, commentaries, basic doctrine and Christian living. Our children's books are also published in this imprint.

Mentor focuses on books written at a level suitable for Bible College and seminary students, pastors, and other serious readers. The imprint includes commentaries, doctrinal studies, examination of current issues and church history.

Christian Heritage contains classic writings from the past.

Christian Focus Publications, Ltd
Geanies House, Fearn, Ross-shire,
IV20 1TW, Scotland, United Kingdom
www.christianfocus.com